PAR AVI
BY AIR N

Cover illustration by Marie-Louise Gay. Endpapers by Robert Macfarlane and Jackie Morris. Illustration above by Tobias Hickey. Title page illustration by Alida Bothma. Copyright © 2019 by the individual illustrators and authors. The Migrations Project was initiated by Piet Grobler and Tobias Hickey of the International Centre for the Picture Book in Society, University of Worcester. All rights reserved. No part of this book may be reproduced, transmitted, or stored in an information retrieval system in any form or by any means, graphic, electronic, or mechanical, including photocopying, taping, and recording, without prior written permission from the publisher. First U.S. edition 2019. First published by Otter-Barry Books (United Kingdom) 2019. Library of Congress Catalog Card Number pending. ISBN 978-1-5362-0961-7. This book was typeset in Gill Sans. Candlewick Studio, an imprint of Candlewick Press, 99 Dover Street, Somerville, Massachusetts 02144 visit us at www.candlewickstudio.com
Printed in Dongguan, Guangdong, China. 19 20 21 22 23 24 TLF 10 9 8 7 6 5 4 3 2 1

MIGRATIONS
Open Hearts, Open Borders

Edited by the International Centre for the Picture Book in Society

an imprint of Candlewick Press

Contents

The images here are a selection from the hundreds sent in by children's book illustrators from all over the world for an exhibition entitled *Migrations*. Its aim is to express support for and solidarity with the hundreds of thousands of human migrants who face immense difficulties and dangers in their struggle to find a better and safer place to live.

Shaun Tan writes:

All migration is an act of imagination, a flight of imagination. A hope that frequently exercises a previously unknown human potential. Migration is also an act of imagination that all too often ends in despair, from death at sea to psychological trauma due to the intolerance of host communities, ignorant hostility, poverty, and illness. What can be done? The universe of stars looks down but does not even ask this question. That's for us, the living, the thinking and feeling: descendants through millennia of successful migration whose ancestors dreamed of something better as they fled across deserts and oceans and ice bridges. It's left for us to imagine what to do, to pass on the dividends of hope that have been invested in us.

Can small gestures—a picture, a friendly message—make a difference? By creating, looking, asking questions, confronting despair, we invest back into an economy far greater than any stock exchange, far nobler than any political system. We help sustain the will to imagine a better world, for adults and especially children, for whom the positive inspiration of art and story can never be overestimated. Like the arctic tern setting out for a new nest some 12,400 mi./20,000 km away, flying through darkness with only the thinnest of magnetic songs for bearings, the migrant moves into the unknown, which holds both promises and fears. Should the imagination of some falter and weaken, whether that of the migrant or the host community, then it must help to look upon the thousands of other shapes just beyond our wingtips, flying in vast formation, and know that we will never be alone.

Migrations, *an exhibition of the International Centre for the Picture Book in Society, was first shown at BIBIANA in Bratislava, Slovakia, in September 2017. The ICPBS, founded at the University of Worcester, England, by Piet Grobler and Tobias Hickey, emphasizes and celebrates the power of illustration to engage with society, particularly by focusing on issues of cultural diversity and the inclusion of minorities and socially disenfranchised people.*

Passenger Pigeon

Diek Grobler, South Africa

Departures

To: Migrations
Taz Lovejoy
Digital Arts Centre
University of Worcester
Henwick Grove
Worcester
WR2 6AJ, U.K.

* Where there is change
there is hope.
Where there is hope
there is life.

Where there is change
there is hope.

Where there is hope
there is life.

Shaun Tan, Australia

DIGITAL ARTS CENTRE
UNIVERSITY OF
WORCESTER
HENWICK GROVE
WORCESTER
UK   WR2 6AJ

Jon Klassen, Canada/USA

A migração mais comum
nas aves é a fuga sazonal
ao inverno, ao frio e à
falta de alimento. É
talvez a melhor metáfora
para o movimento migra-
tório dos refugiados:
outra fuga, e não um
abandono permanente.
Que tal como os pássaros,
os migrantes encontrem
a primavera onde quer
que cheguem. E também
nos lugares de onde parti-
ram, se quiserem voltar.

To:
MiGRATIONS exhibition
(ICPBS illustration)
Digital Arts Centre
University of Worcester
Henwick Grove
Worcester
WR2 6AJ
United Kingdom

Birds migrate in a seasonal escape from winter, with its cold and lack of food. And perhaps a better way to see the migration of refugees is as another escape, not a permanent departure. Like the birds, the migrants find spring wherever they come. And [hopefully] also in the place they left, if they should ever wish to return.

17

Catarina Sobral, Portugal

In the end
we only regret
the chances we
didn't take.
It begins with
a single step...

MIGRATIONS EXHIBITION
TAZ LOVEJOY
DIGITAL ARTS CENTRE
UNIVERSITY OF WORCESTER
HENWICK GROVE
WORCESTER
WR2 6AJ

Rhian Wyn Harrison 2017

In the end we only regret the chances we didn't take.
It begins with a single step . . .

Rhian Wyn Harrison, UK

Fly and flow.

21

Alessandra Cimatoribus, Italy

Beyond the clouds, rain and mountains . . .

Yuval Zommer, UK

25

Katerina Dubovik, Belarus

Vše je možné.
Narodil jsi se
volný.

Everything is
possible.
You were born
free. LOVE from
Petr Horáček

Royal Mail
proud to support
Stroke
association

Migration exhibition
Taz Lovejoy
Digital Arts Centre
University of Worcester
WR2 6AJ

Everything is possible.
You were born free.

27

Petr Horáček, Czech Republic/UK

Kana Okita, Japan

Hope!

Long Journeys

As free from danger as the heavens are free
From pain and toil, there would they build and be,
And sail about the world to scenes unheard
Of and unseen — O, were they but a bird!

John Clare

31

Becky Palmer, UK

27 June   2017

THE SKIES HAVE
No BORDERS,   MIGRATIONS exhibition
TAZ   LoVEJoY
From   christopher corr   DIGITAL ARTs   CENTRE
University of Worcester
Henwick   Grove
Worcester
W R 2   6AJ

The skies have no borders.

33   Christopher Corr, UK

"We are all travellers in the wilderness of this world, and the best we can find in our travels is an honest friend."

Robert Louis Stevenson

34

35   Andy Robert Davies, UK

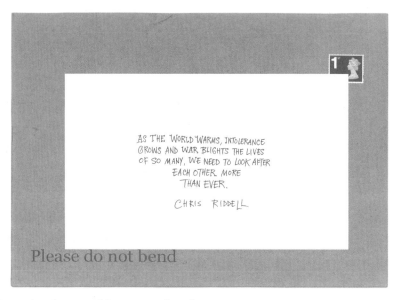

As the world warms, intolerance
grows and war blights the lives
of so many, we need to look after
each other more
than ever.

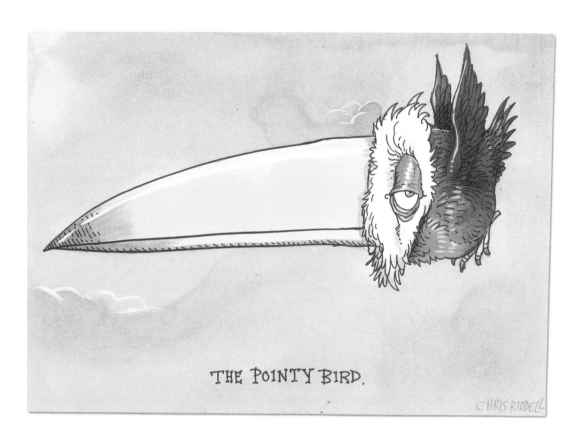

THE POINTY BIRD.

Chris Riddell, UK

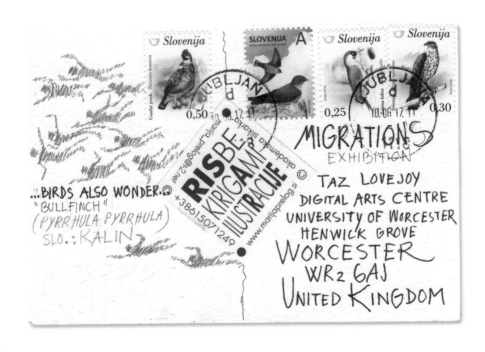

Birds also wonder . . .

39

Marija Prelog, Slovenia

No importa de donde
vengas, ni tus colores o
a donde llegues, siempre
existirá alguien de
buen corazón dispuesto
a ayudarte.
Sólo ten un buen viaje!

———

Patricia González Palacios
Santiago - chile

MSG:
Exhibition
TAZ LOVEJOY
DiGiTAL ARTS CENTRE
UNIVERSITY OF WORCESTER
HENWICK GROVE
WORCESTER
WR2 GAJ
UNITED KINGDOM.

No matter where you come from, what color you are,
or where you come to, there will always be someone
of good heart to help you.
Only travel safely!

41   Patricia González Palacios, Chile

I think we are finally going somewhere safe . . .

43

Leila Ajiri, Germany

«Fly high!»

FROM: KSENIA
Efimova
Russia, St. Petersburg

To: Migrations
exhibition (ICPBS
Illustration)
Digital Arts Centre
University of Worcester
Henwick Grove
Worcester WR2 6AJ
United Kingdom

Fly high!

Ksenia Efimova, Russia

BIRDS FLY

Some with one leg
Some with one eye
Some with one heart

MIGRATIONS exhibition
Taz Lovejoy
Digital Arts Centre
University of Worcester
Henwick Grove
Worcester
WR2 6AJ

Jungtine Karalystė

ROMB-BOMB.COM
FACEBOOK.COM/
ILLUSTRATEDTEXTILE

PIRMENYBINĖ
PRIORITAIRE

Birds fly
Some with one leg
Some with one eye
Some with one heart

'FLY BY NIGHT'

by Neal Layton

for the

MIGRATIONS

EXHIBITION

pencil, ink and collage digitally
combined with some hand colouring

TO

TA2 LOVEJOY

DIGITAL ARTS CENTRE

UNIVERSITY OF WORCESTER

HENWICK GROVE

WORCESTER

WR2 6AJ

U.K.

'Fly by Night'

Neal Layton, UK

Saviour says: "Be nice."
(What's so difficult about that?)

Inga Grimm, Sweden

I fly alone during the night looking for a place to carry on my life.
The swallow

Travel well!

53

María León, Spain

It's that dream that we carry with us
that something wonderful will happen,
that it has to happen,
that time will open,
that the heart will open,
that doors will open,
that the mountains will open,
that wells will leap up,
that the dream will open,
that one morning we'll slip in
to a harbor that we've never known.

"Det er den Draumen" by Olav H. Hauge
translated by Robert Bly

Stian Hole, Norway

From: Satoko Watanabe

To: MIGRATIONS exhibition
(ICPBS Illustration)
Digital Arts Center
University of Worcester
Henwick Grove
Worcester WR 2 6 AJ

United Kingdom

VIA AIR MAIL

A little bird flies in the sky.
A little bird is damaged.
A little bird needs a place to take a rest.

A little bird flies in the sky.
A little bird is damaged.
A little bird needs a place to take a rest.

Jul. 2017

SATOKO WATANABE

Satoko Watanabe, Japan

The albatross holds in its eye, the
                                    storm
And, over more miles than lie between
                   us and the moon,
The small green island of its home.

                                Taz Lovejoy

Words and picture come with   Digital Arts Centre
love from   University of Worcester
Nicola Davies   Henwick Grove
Wales   Worcester
                                  WR 2 6 AJ

The Langton · 300g/m² · 140lb Cold Pressed · NOT
                www. nicola-davies. com

The albatross holds in its eye the storm
And, over more miles than lie between us and the moon,
The small green island of its home.

59

Nicola Davies, UK

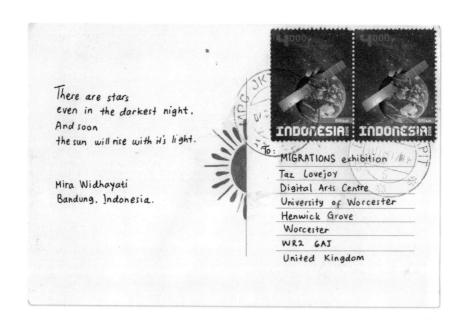

There are stars
even in the darkest night.
And soon
the sun will rise with its light.

61

Mira Widhayati, Indonesia

Axel Scheffler, UK

Borders — not what they used to be

Arrivals

"From up here I see no borders."

Natalia Gurovich, Chile/Mexico

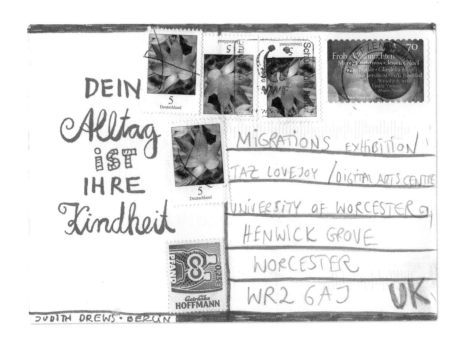

DEIN
Alltag
ist
IHRE
Kindheit

MIGRATIONS EXHIBITION /
TAZ LOVEJOY / DIGITAL ARTS CENTRE
UNIVERSITY OF WORCESTER
HENWICK GROVE
WORCESTER
WR2 6AJ   UK

JUDITH DREWS · BERLIN

Your everyday is their childhood.

Judith Drews, Germany

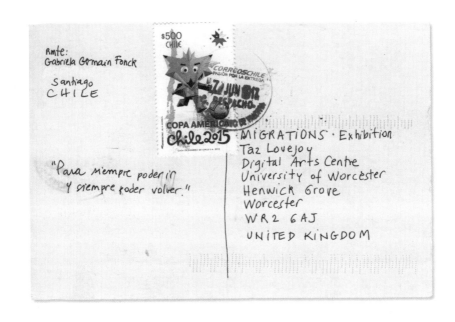

"One can always go and one can always return."

SIEMPRE PODER IR
SIEMPRE PODER VOLVER

69   Gabriela Germain Fonck, Chile

To.

Piet Grobler C/o Mr Marian Potrok
MIGRATIONS- project
International Center for the Picture Book in Society
c/o BIBIANA, Medzinárodný dom umenia pre deti
Panská ul. 41,
815 39 Bratislava
Slovakia

Open the door.

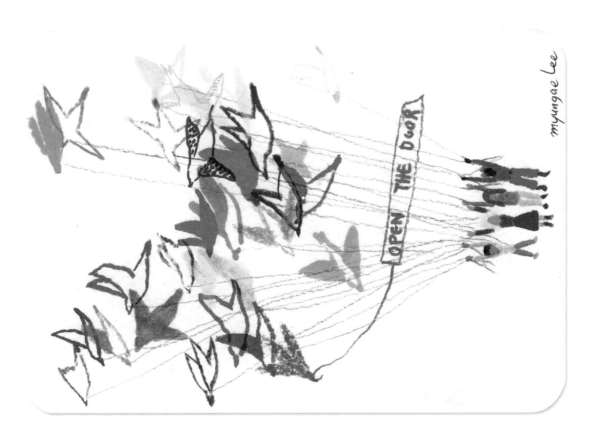

OPEN THE DOOR

myungae lee

Myungae Lee, South Korea

My dream for everyone all around the globe is to have
a legendary bird that can fly to wherever that they love
to travel, without fear.
Having a good life is everyone's right. So try to make
these wishes become reality.

73   Mohammad Barrangi Fashtami, Iran

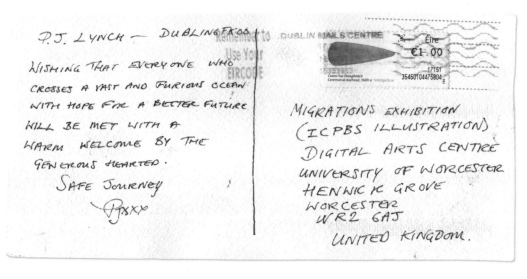

P.J. LYNCH — DUBLIN GFX00

WISHING THAT EVERYONE WHO
CROSSES A VAST AND FURIOUS OCEAN
WITH HOPE FOR A BETTER FUTURE
WILL BE MET WITH A
WARM WELCOME BY THE
GENEROUS HEARTED.
SAFE JOURNEY
PJxxx

MIGRATIONS EXHIBITION
(ICPBS ILLUSTRATION)
DIGITAL ARTS CENTRE
UNIVERSITY OF WORCESTER
HENWICK GROVE
WORCESTER
WR2 6AJ
UNITED KINGDOM.

Wishing that everyone who crosses a vast
and furious ocean with hope for a better future
will be met with a warm welcome by the generous hearted.
Safe journey.

P.J. Lynch, Ireland

May 31st 2017
Imagination and knowledge, words and ideas fly over fences, barbed wire, brick walls, through prison bars, stormy skies and borders....

Marie-Louise Gay (Canada)

. { MIGRATIONS Exhibition
. { Digital Arts Centre
. { University of Worcester
. { Henwick Grove
. { Worcester
. { WR2 6AJ
. { United Kingdom

Imagination and knowledge, words and ideas
fly over fences, barbed wire, brick walls,
through prison bars, stormy skies and borders . . .

Marie-Louise Gay, Canada

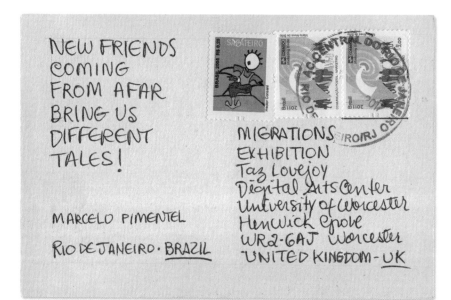

New friends coming from afar
bring us different tales!

Marcelo Pimentel, Brazil

PRIORITY

Helena Bergendahl, Sweden

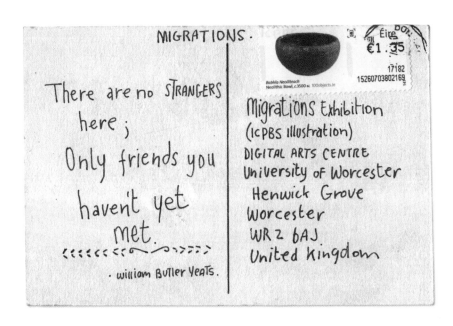

There are no strangers here;
Only friends you haven't yet met.

Ascribed to William Butler Yeats

Brian Fitzer, Ireland

All the Children of the World Should Feel Safe and Cherished

Mies van Hout

Mies van Hout, Netherlands

84

Hope for the Future

godspeed.

I wish you
well upon your
way.

To: Migrations exhibition
D.A.C. Illustration
UNIVERSITY OF WORCESTER
HENWICK Grove
WORCESTER
WR2 6AJ
UNited KingdoM

FROM PIET GROBLER

Godspeed.
I wish you well upon your way.

Piet Grobler, South Africa

We are one!

Nelleke Verhoeff, Netherlands

THE SPAN OF THE EARTH

IS OUR

LIMTLESS

EXPANSION

ROGER MELLO

ADDRESS to:
PIET GROBLER
c/o MR. MARIAN POTROK
MIGRATIONS - PROJECT
INTERNATIONAL CENTER FOR
THE PICTURE BOOK IN SOCIETY
c/o BIBIANA
MEDZINÁRODNÝ DOM
UMENIA PRE DETI
PANSKÁ UL. 41,
815 39 BRATISLAVA
SLOVAKIA

The span of the earth is our limitless expansion.

Roger Mello, Brazil

COMPARTIR
EL MUNDO
EN PAZ Y
LIBERTAD.
LA TIERRA
Y LAS PERSONAS
NO TIENEN
DUEÑO.

ISOL

MIGRATIONS
exhibition
Taz Lovejoy
Digital Arts Centre
University of Worcester
Henwick Grove
WORCESTER
WR2 6AJ
UNITED KINGDOM

Share the world in peace and freedom.
The earth and its people have no owners.

life is MOVEMENT

ISOL

Isol, Argentina

one day, it will
be better.
Stay strong.
You are
welcome.

Maral Sassouni

MIGRATIONS exhibition
c/o Taz Lovejoy
DIGITAL ARTS CENTRE
UNIVERSITY of WORCESTER
HENWICK GROVE
WORCESTER   WR2 6AJ
UNITED KINGDOM

One day it will be better.
Stay strong.
You are welcome.

95

Maral Sassouni, USA

I came to UK as a refugee in 1993 because of the war in my country, Bosnia and Herzegovina. In my suitcase I had eleven paintbrushes. I thought they would help me to survive in my new life. Now I am a glass artist, have my safe nest (studio) and am making little birds out of melted glass.

97 Maya Stanic, Bosnia and Herzegovina/UK

"Wherever you go becomes
a part of you
somehow"
— Anita Desai

From: Renate Rogina
Latvia

To:
MIGRATIONS
exhibition
(ICPBS illustration)
Digital Arts Centre
University of Worcester
Henwick Grove
Worcester
WR2 6AJ
United Kingdom

R LATVIJAS PASTS
RR 543769735 LV

"Wherever you go becomes
a part of you somehow."

Anita Desai

Renate Logina, Latvia

Simurgh&30 Kids :

Simurgh is a Persian legendary and mythical
bird, the symbol of wisdom and unity. It decided
to collect 30 kids from all over the world, lead them
to the mount Qaf and learn them wisdom, knowledge,
humanity and goodness to build a better world.

AMIR.SH
2017

Simurgh is a Persian legendary and mythical bird, the symbol of wisdom and unity. It decided to collect 30 kids from all over the world, lead them to the mount Qaf and learn them wisdom, knowledge, humanity and goodness to build a better world.

Amir Shabanipour, Iran

FROM:
moya Takahashi

DEAR:
MIGRATIONS Exhibiton

Tal Lovejoy
Digital Art Center
University of Worcester

Henwick Grove
Worcester WR26AT
United Kingdom

AIR MAIL

We hope peace.

Mogu Takahashi, Japan

"Hope" is the thing with feathers—
That perches in the soul—
And sings the tune without
    the words—
And never stops—at all—

And sweetest—in the Gale—
    is heard—
And sore must be the storm—
That could abash the little Bird
That kept so many warm—

I've heard it in the chillest land—
And on the strangest Sea—
Yet, never, in Extremity,
It asked a crumb—of Me.

Emily Dickinson

Jane Ray, UK

LEILA AJIRI, originally from Iran, now lives in Kreis Bergstrasse, Germany, where she is a professional artist and a prominent participant in promoting the integration of migrants in the community.

HELENA BERGENDAHL was born in Gothenburg, Sweden. She has illustrated many books for children and has served on the international jury for the Biennial of Illustrations, Bratislava.

ALIDA BOTHMA lives in Greyton, South Africa. Among her international awards are a merit award and a bronze medal from the UNESCO Noma Concours in Tokyo.

ALESSANDRA CIMATORIBUS was born in Friuli, Italy. Her books have been translated into sixteen languages, and her murals at Philadelphia Zoo received the Association of Zoos and Aquariums 2014 Exhibit Award.

KATERINA DUBOVIK is an illustrator and designer who was born in Minsk, Belarus, and now lives in Amsterdam.

CHRISTOPHER CORR is a Londoner who studied at the Royal College of Art and still lives in the city. But a love of travel inspires his work, which, he says, "is all about joy, color, and a love of life."

ANDY ROBERT DAVIES studied illustration at Loughborough University, UK. He is an illustration lecturer and professional illustrator for children's and adult books and magazines. He lives in Malvern, UK.

NICOLA DAVIES has written many books for children about nature and wildlife and is an accomplished artist in her own right. She was named Writer in Residence for 2018–2019 at Book Trust.

JUDITH DREWS has had her work published in more than seventeen countries, and she was a member of the nominating body for the Astrid Lindgren Memorial Award from 2008 to 2015. She lives in Berlin, Germany.

KSENIA EFIMOVA writes: "I am a mostly self-taught artist. Currently I am studying at a school of digital art in Saint Petersburg, upgrading my skills. I am also working as a freelance illustrator."

MOHAMMAD BARRANGI FASHTAMI writes: "I am both an artist and an athlete. I have a disability in my left hand, though I believe it is by no means a stymying limitation. Born in Rasht, a northern city in Iran, I love printmaking. I make them with my hand and using my leg."

BRIAN FITZER is the pen name of Brian Fitzgerald. His wordless book *Bounce Bounce* won the international Silent Book Contest in 2014. He lives in Dublin.

GABRIELA GERMAIN FONCK studied drawing and design at Valparaiso Catholic University, Chile, and is a freelance illustrator and author. Her most recent book is *Cuando el viento sopla fuerte.*

STEPHEN FOWLER specializes in rubber stamping and alternative printmaking. He graduated from St. Martin's School of Art in London and is a lecturer at Worcester University's Institute of the Arts.

MARIE-LOUISE GAY was born in Québec City, Canada. Her work as an author and illustrator has earned many distinctions, including the Governor General's Literary Award and the E. B. White Read-Aloud Award, and has been selected for the International Board on Books for Young People Honor List.

INGA GRIMM was born in 1969 in Tübingen, Germany, and has lived in Sweden since 1998. A self-taught artist, she creates colorful assemblages as well as graphic works.

DIEK GROBLER likes to depict "little disasters and small miracles." Born in South Africa, he has been exhibiting his work since 1988. His work extends from fine art to animation and has been shown in Beijing, Edinburgh, Prague, Venice, and many other cities.

PIET GROBLER is an award-winning South African illustrator with degrees in theology, journalism, and visual arts (illustration). After nine years lecturing in the UK, he returned to South Africa to be a freelance illustrator again. He is a visiting professor in illustration at the University of Worcester, UK.

NATALIA GUROVICH studied graphic design at the Universidad Católica de Chile and is currently a freelance illustrator in Mexico City. She has received numerous international awards and illustrated more than twenty books. Her latest, *El maestro no ha venido,* was awarded the 2017 Special Prize for children's book illustration at the International Book Fair in Novi Sad, Serbia.

RHIAN WYN HARRISON lives in South Devon, UK. She was a typographer and graphic designer and is now "a born-again artist" specializing in mixed-media illustration.

TOBIAS HICKEY is a course leader in illustration at the University of Worcester, UK. He studied graphic design at Liverpool Polytechnic and illustration at St. Martin's School of Art, and his images are often seen in newspapers and magazines as well as in children's books. With Piet Grobler, he is a founder of ICPBS.

STIAN HOLE is one of Norway's leading graphic designers and illustrators of children's books. His book *Garmann's Summer* won an Ezra Jack Keats New Writer Award and Germany's Children's Literature Award. He lives in Oslo.

PETR HORÁČEK was born in Prague and now lives in the UK. Since winning the Books for Children Newcomer Award in 2001, he has had many honors, including being short-listed for the Royal Society Young People's Book Prize 2017 for *A First Book of Animals.*

MIES VAN HOUT was born in Eindhoven, Netherlands, and has been illustrating children's books for around thirty years. *Vrolijk* won a Vlag en Wimpel award in 2014.

ISOL is the pen name of Marisol Misenta. Her contributions to children's literature gained her a Golden Apple Award in 2003

and the Astrid Lindgren Memorial Award in 2013. She lives in Buenos Aires.

JON KLASSEN has won both the American Caldecott Medal and the British Kate Greenaway Medal for children's book illustration. Born in Winnipeg, Canada, he currently lives in Los Angeles.

NEAL LAYTON was born in Chichester, UK, and now lives in Portsmouth. His book *The Story of Stars* won the School Library Association Information Book Award for 2014.

MYUNGAE LEE studied painting in college. Her first book, *Plastic Island* (2015), gained honors at the Bologna Children's Book Fair, the Nami Island International Picture Book Illustration Concours, and the Biennial of Illustrations Bratislava.

MARÍA LEÓN is a Spanish artist who describes herself as "an enthusiastic biologist who likes to observe nature and paint around that." Born in A Coruña, she lives in Tarifa, Spain.

RENATE LOGINA lives in Riga, Latvia, and is a graduate of the Art Academy of Latvia. A freelance illustrator, she is an expert in the games field as well as in traditional media.

P. J. LYNCH is a winner of the Mother Goose Award and the Kate Greenaway Medal (twice). He was Ireland's Laureate na nÓg for 2016–2018 and lives in Dublin.

ROBERT MACFARLANE is a fellow of Emmanuel College, Cambridge. His books on mountains, landscapes, and travel have won many awards and have been published in more than twenty countries. With Jackie Morris, he is author of *The Lost Words.*

ROGER MELLO has illustrated more than one hundred books and written twenty-two. He has won many international prizes and awards, including the 2014 Hans Christian Andersen Award for Illustration. Born in Brasilia, he now lives in Rio de Janeiro.

JACKIE MORRIS has written and illustrated many books. Her sensitivity to the natural world shines in her work, including her illustrations for *The Lost Words,* chosen by British booksellers as the most beautiful book of 2017. She lives in Pembrokeshire, Wales.

KANA OKITA is a freelance artist and graphic designer. A graduate of Musashino Art University, she lives in Tokyo.

PATRICIA GONZÁLEZ PALACIOS has been exhibiting her work in her homeland of Chile and in Spain since 1982. She is both an independent artist and a teacher of illustration.

BECKY PALMER graduated from the Cambridge School of Art in 2012. Her first graphic novel was published in France in 2014. Most recently, she illustrated *Ellie and Lump's Very Busy Day* by Dorothy Clarke. She teaches children's book illustration at Anglia Ruskin University.

MARCELO PIMENTEL, born in Rio de Janeiro, is one of Brazil's leading illustrators. His wordless book *O Fim da Fila* (*The End of the Line*) won the Grand Prix at the Nami Island Concours in 2015.

MARIJA PRELOG gained her diploma at the Academy of Graphic Arts in Ljubljana, Slovenia, and though she still lives in the city, she says that nature is her greatest source of inspiration for her many picture books and other works.

JANE RAY was born in London and studied art and design at Middlesex University. Since 1989 she has illustrated more than fifty books and written several. Winner of a Smarties Award in 1992,

she has been short-listed for the Kate Greenaway Medal six times.

CHRIS RIDDELL is both a leading children's illustrator and writer and an acclaimed political cartoonist. Among his many awards are a UNESCO Prize for Children's Literature and three Kate Greenaway Medals. He was UK Children's Laureate from 2013 to 2017. He lives in Brighton, UK.

ROMB-BOMB.COM is a Lithuanian online gallery of textile designs and artifacts using historic and natural Baltic motifs, run by Gabrielius Mackevicius.

MARAL SASSOUNI grew up in Playa del Rey, California, and studied design and animation at UCLA. Since 1999 she has been based primarily in Paris. Her first book, *The Green Umbrella,* was a Bank Street College Best Children's Book of the Year in 2017.

AXEL SCHEFFLER was born in Hamburg, Germany, and now lives in London. Since 1988 he has illustrated some of the world's best-loved children's books, including Julia Donaldson's *The Gruffalo,* which won the Smarties Prize in 1999. Their latest is *The Ugly Five* (2017).

AMIR SHABANIPOUR is a painter and illustrator living in Rasht, Iran. He was a Selected Artist for the Illustrarte Award 2016, and his work has been exhibited at the Bologna Children's Book Fair.

CATARINA SOBRAL was born in Coimbra, Portugal, and now lives in Lisbon. A writer as well as an illustrator, she won the Bologna Children's Book Fair International Award for Illustration in 2014.

MAYA STANIC grew up in Bosnia-Herzegovina and has a master's degree in product design from Sarajevo University. Now based in London, she creates fine work in stained glass seen in many locations.

MOGU TAKAHASHI lives and works in Tokyo. Since 2006 his work has been exhibited and published in many countries.

SHAUN TAN grew up in Perth, Australia, and has gained worldwide acclaim as an illustrator and filmmaker. In 2011 he received the Astrid Lindgren Memorial Award for his contribution to children's literature.

NELLEKE VERHOEFF lives in Rotterdam, Netherlands. She began as a performer but found her true vocation in art and illustration. *Concerto* was a finalist in the 2018 Silent Book Contest.

SATOKO WATANABE was born in Kyoto, Japan, and studied oil painting and printing at Kyoto Seika University. He lives in Saitama, Japan.

MIRA WIDHAYATI studied visual communication design at Bandung Institute of Technology, Indonesia, and is a member of Kelompok Pencinta Bacaan Anak, the Society for the Advancement of Children's Literature.

YUVAL ZOMMER is a graduate of the Royal College of Art, London, and renowned for children's books that put the living world at the heart of storytelling. His *Big Book of Beasts* won the English Association 4-11 Book Award in 2018.

ACKNOWLEDGMENTS

Grateful thanks are due to all the artists who contributed their works and to the International Board on Books for Young People (IBBY) for its support. Also to Robert Bly for permission to use his translation of "Det er den Draumen" and to Miranda Otter-Barry Ross for translations from Spanish. The text of Emily Dickinson's "Hope" is from *The Poems of Emily Dickinson*, edited by Thomas H. Johnson and published by the Belknap Press of Harvard University Press. Every effort has been made to trace copyright holders of texts quoted from. If any copyright items have been inadvertently included, the publishers will be glad to be informed and to make acknowledgment in any future edition.

Peregrine is pilgrim-bird — world-wanderer, cloud-splitter

Ever looked up, seen peregrine

Race sun across the sky, leave light for dust?

Ever wondered what it must be like to

Ghost over borders, as peregrine does?

Rise from ground now, up by quick wing-flicks and gyre

Into air, where frontiers fade fast.

Never stop dreaming of flying further, higher,

Ending up where the heart hopes for, longs for, at last.

Robert Macfarlane and Jackie Morris, UK